A Kwanzaa Tale

By

Sonorra C. McMath

In Collaboration with

Breonna Nared

Mosaiah Ndalama

Latricia Jackson

Naylani Hunter

Deshae

fanikia

A Kwanzaa Tale

An Original Publication of My Mom's a Stud Publishing LLC

Copyright 2013 My Mom's a Stud Publishing Company LLC

First Printing 31 December 2013

Printed in the U.S.A.

Dedication

We honor the sacrifices of our ancestors of Rainier Valley, Central District, Skyway, Columbia City, the South end and West Seattle.

This book is dedicated first and foremost to the parents and supporters of the 2013 Kwanzaa Celebration at Life Enrichment Bookstore, located at 5023 Ranier Ave S. Seattle, Washington. Without you we would not have the children and community building that brought this book into existence.

Most importantly, this book is dedicated to Ms Vickie Williams and Aaliyah Messiah. Thank you so very much for your undying efforts, love, commitment, and community support. You are the glue of the community.

"Roots of Knowledge"

ABOUT THE BOOK

This book was created with the input of the children who participated in the 2013 Kwanzaa celebration at Life Enrichment Bookstore on the night of Ujima.

Within one hour the children painted, drew, and created crafts while telling a story they didn't believe they'd see in a book. This book was created as a representation of unity, perseverance, and responsibly (Ujima).

The workbook section at the end of this book is designed to increase self awareness, improve communication, interpersonal skills, self worth, and enhance writing skills.

Proceeds from the sale of this book directly support Life Enrichment Bookstore (Seattle). No assistants/contributors, artists, printers or publishers maintain rights, royalties, or privileges to the story.

We are more powerful than any being alive and we can do anything we set our minds to. It starts with communication and cooperation.

"We Are Black Wall Street"

One love

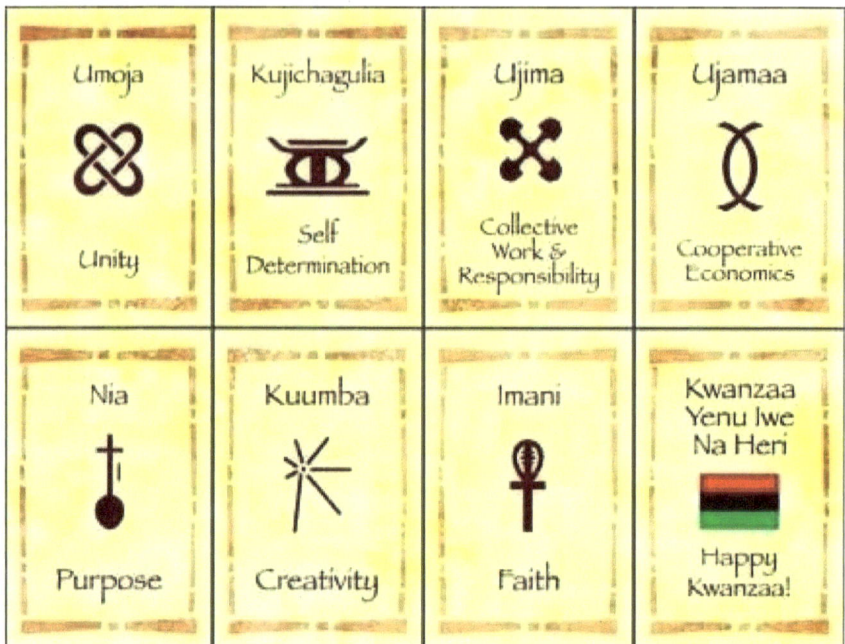

Umoja Unity	Kujichagulia Self Determination	Ujima Collective Work & Responsibility	Ujamaa Cooperative Economics
Nia Purpose	Kuumba Creativity	Imani Faith	Kwanzaa Yenu Iwe Na Heri Happy Kwanzaa!

O Kwanzaa

O Kwanzaa, O Kwanzaa, O Kwanzaa

Kwanzaa.

O Kwanzaa, O Kwanzaa, O Kwanzaa

Kwanzaa.

Seven days of celebration. Nguzo saba.

Seven days of celebration. Habari gani?

Seven days of celebration. Nguzo saba.

Seven days of celebration. Harambee!

O Kwanzaa, O Kwanzaa, O Kwanzaa

Kwanzaa.

O Kwanzaa, O Kwanzaa, O Kwanzaa

Kwanzaa.

In Seattle Washington, tucked away at 5023 Rainier Ave S., there sits a magical place called Life Enrichment Bookstore. All sorts of community events occurred in the building. People would enter and just enjoy one another. Even if they came in sad, they left out happy. Some people say it is touched by the ancestors.

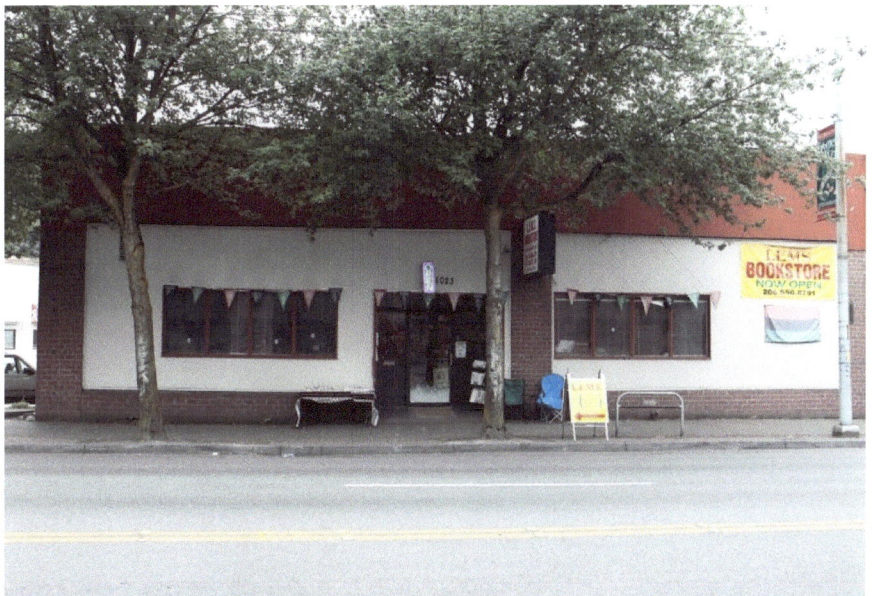

One day, Sonorra walked into the bookstore to share some books and T-shirts.

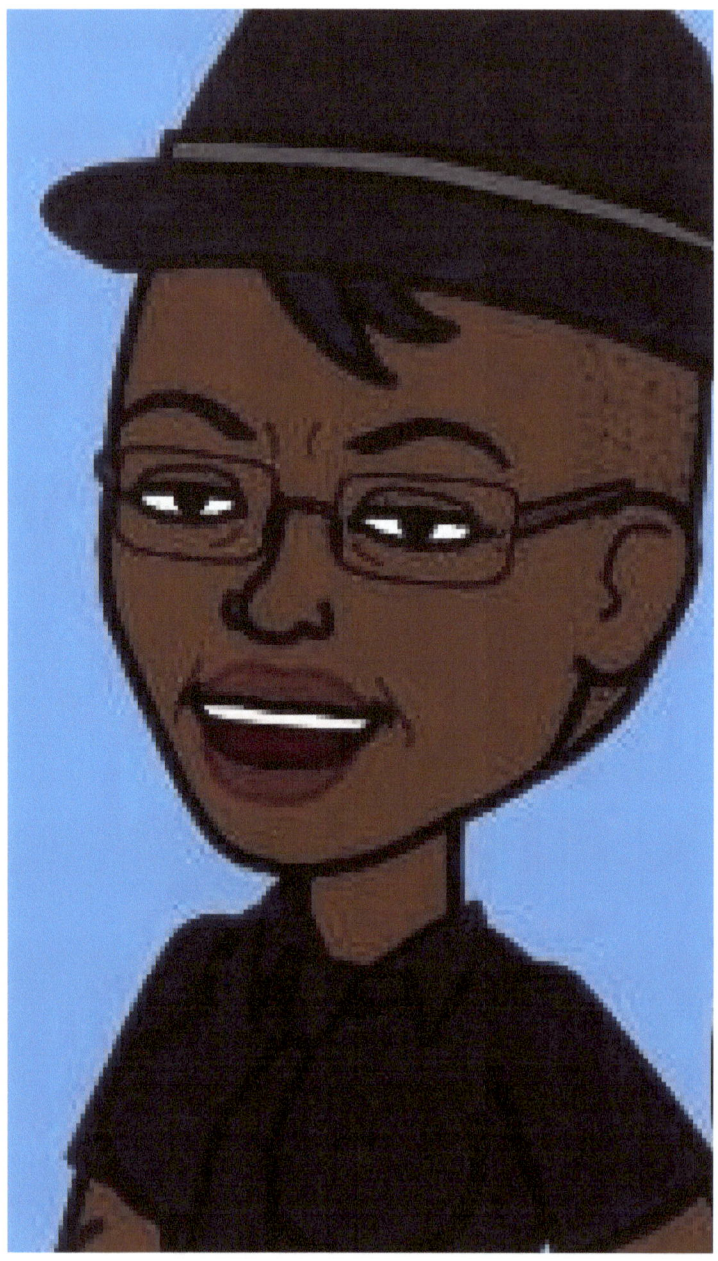

Instead of conducting business, she began making arts, crafts, and t-shirts with the children.

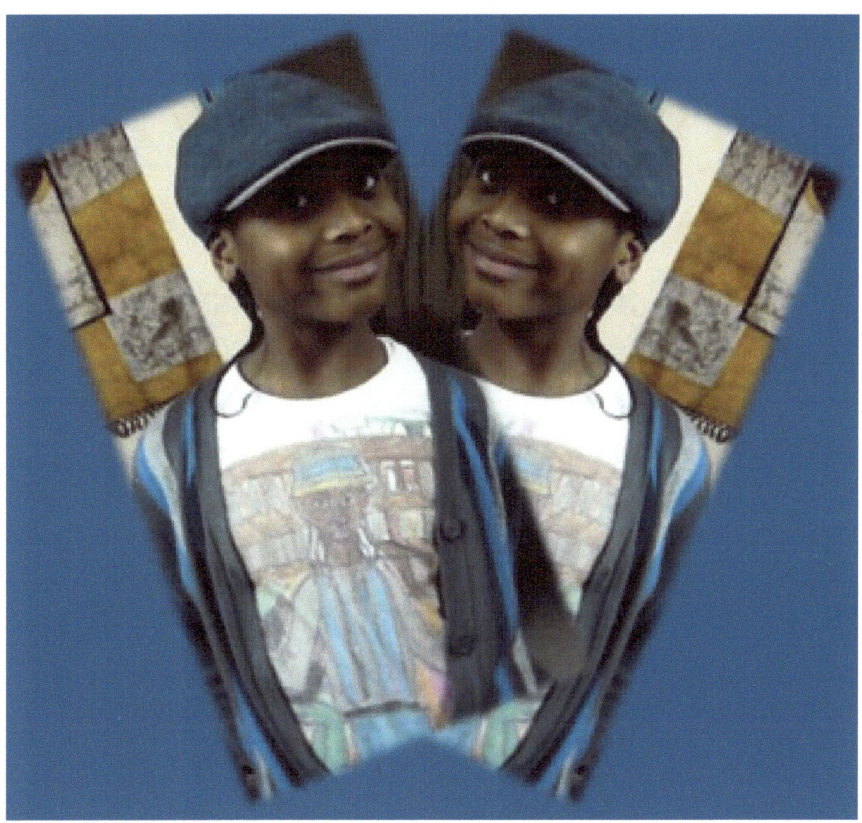

Ms. Vickie, the bookstore owner, noticed the wonderful job Sonorra had done with the children.

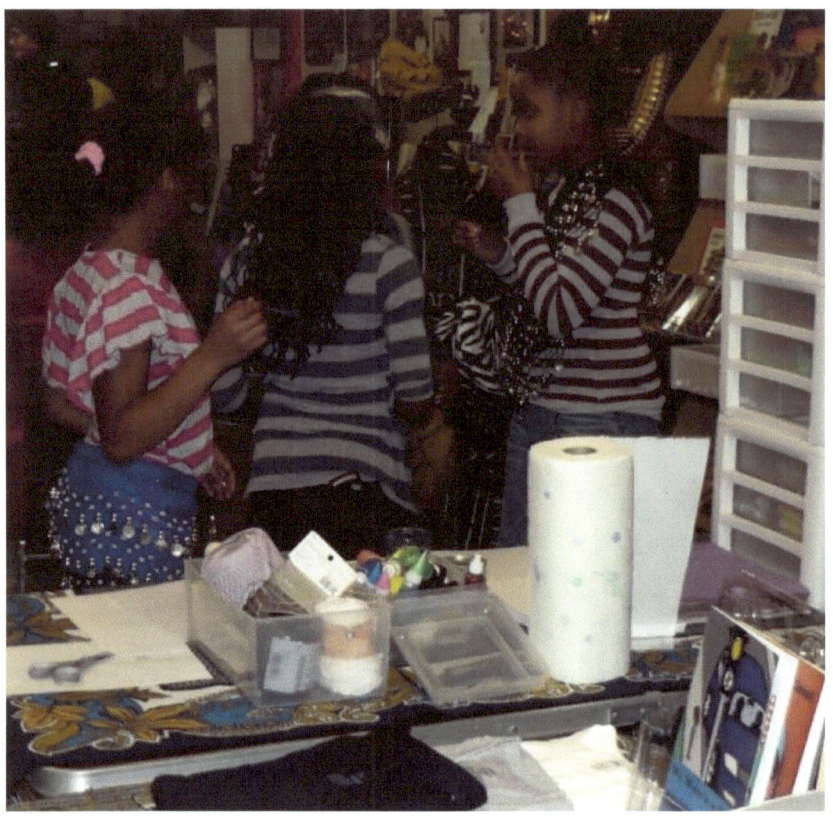

Ms. Vickie approached Sonorra and asked, "Would you like to work with us on the night of Ujima for the Kwanzaa celebration?" We would like you to work with the children."

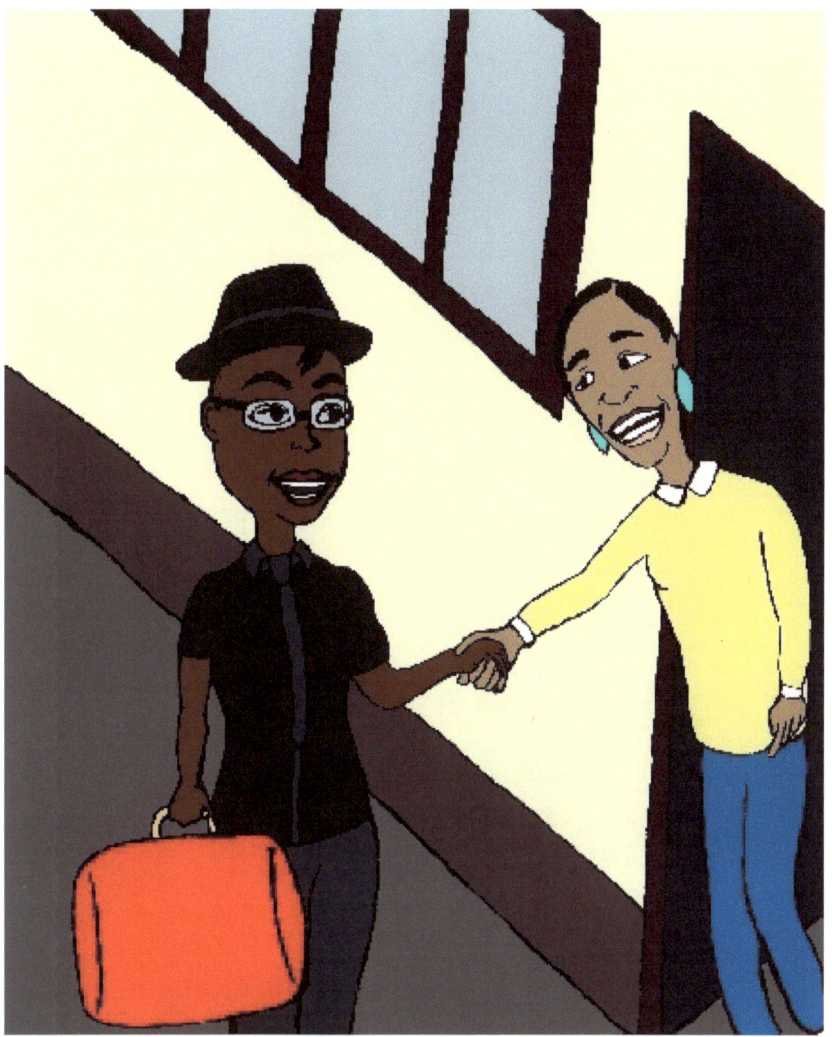

Sonorra did not immediately respond. She was not confident she would serve the community well, because she had no experience planning a Kwanzaa celebration.

On the night of Umoja, Sonorra decided to use her resources, to work with purpose and contribute to the community in the spirit of the ancestors. She hugged Ms. Vickie and agreed to work with the children for Ujima.

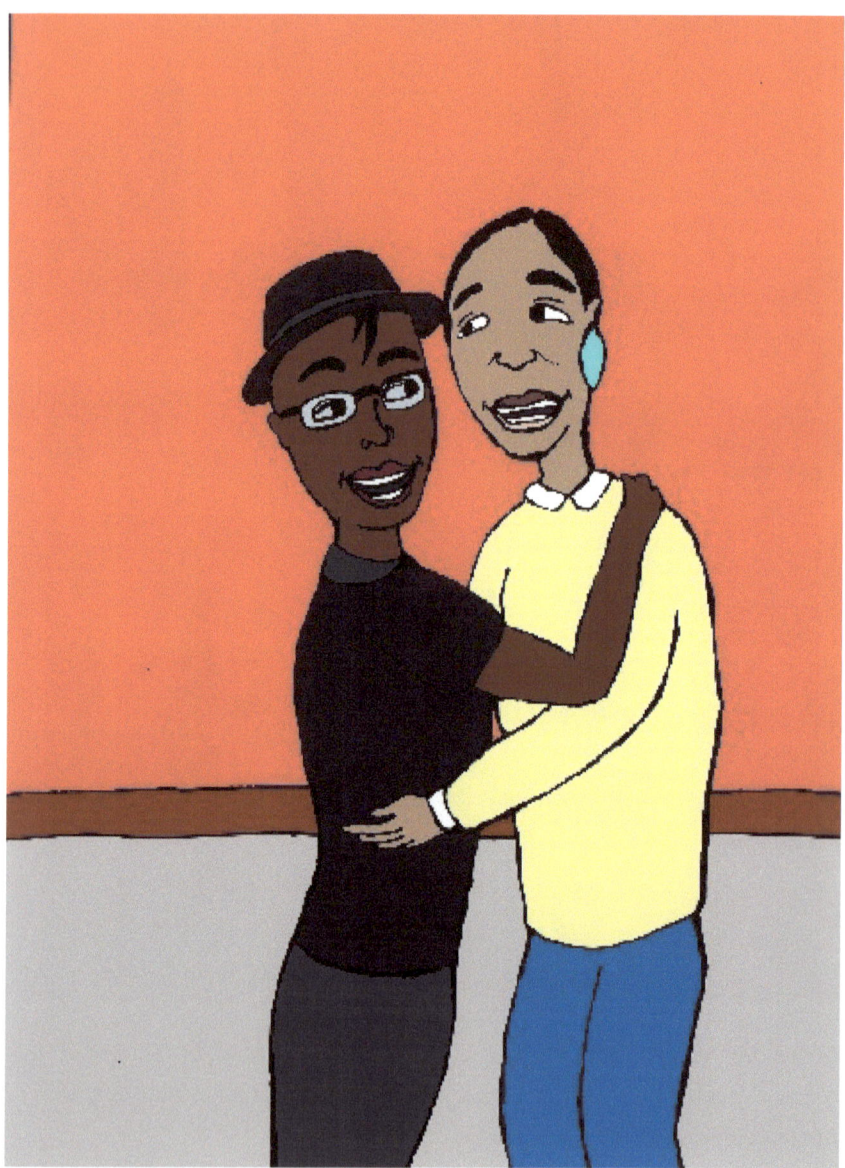

The night of the Ujima celebration had finally come. Sonorra brought in her container of crafts, her printer, and her computer.

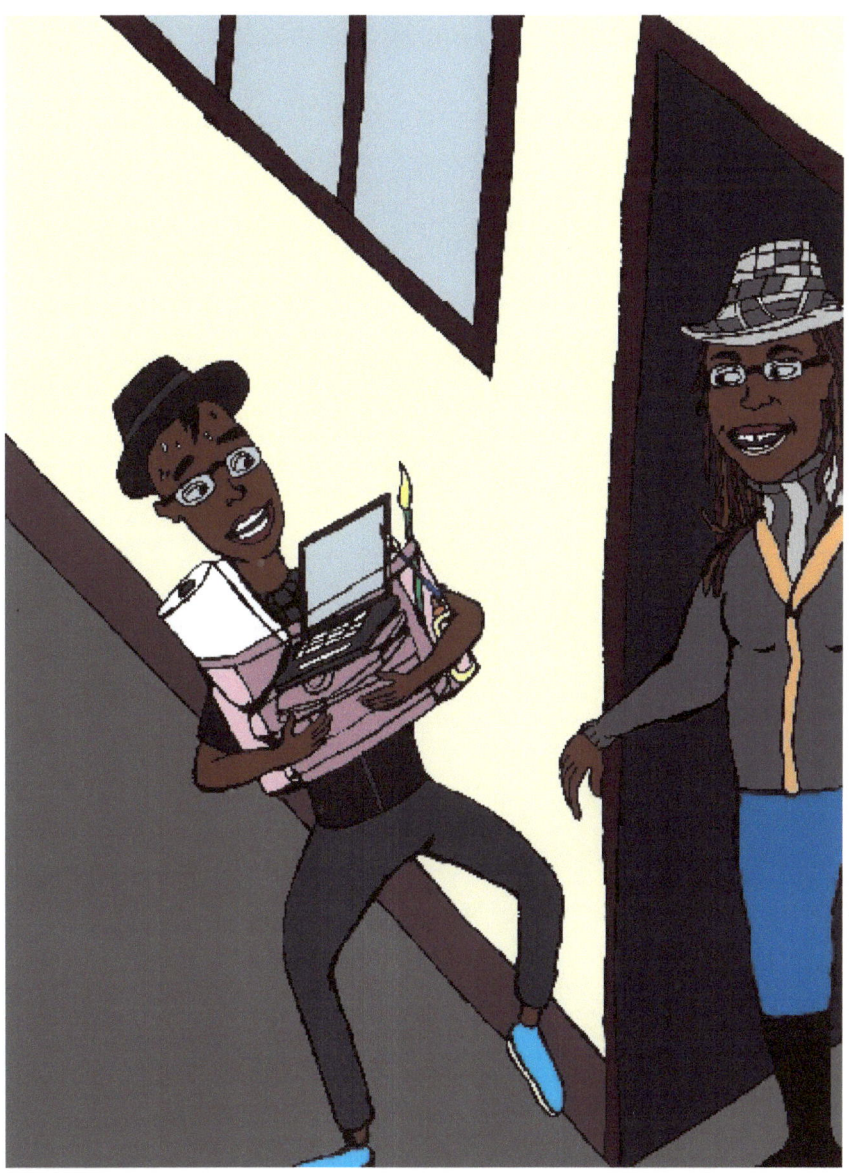

Sonorra said to Ms. Aaliyah "I'll just use my skills to work collectively with the children. We'll talk and work on crafts and we'll write a book collectively."

Ms Aaliyah smiled and said, "That's a fine idea, but we would like you to discuss bullying, domestic violence, and maintaining safe boundaries."

Sonorra smiled nervously. She the project was challenging. Sonorra had to figure out how she was going to combine the beauty of Ujima with the tragedy of community violence. She also knew it was important to ensure the children understood the need to remain safe in an unsafe world.

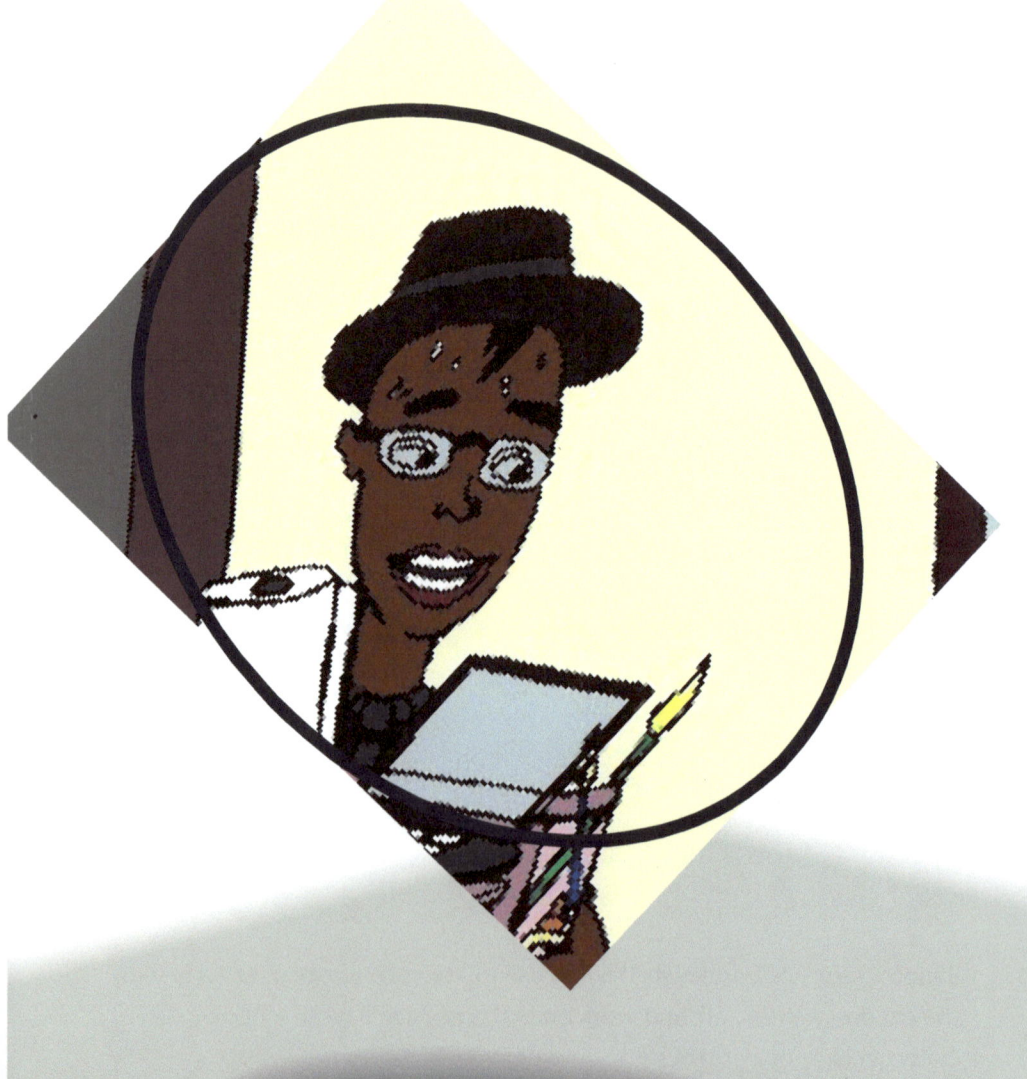

The ceremony began. We sang the Kwanzaa song and the Black National Anthem lead by Ms. Aaliyah.

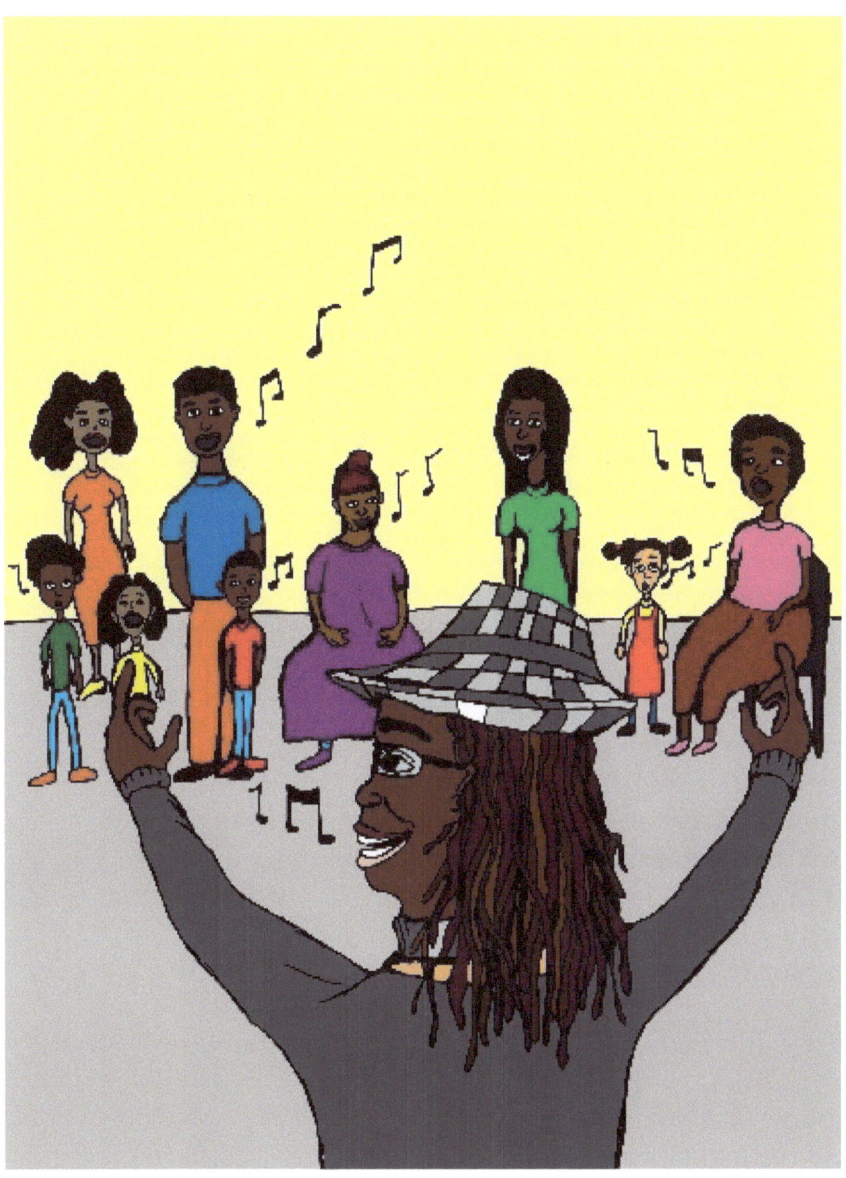

Lift every voice and sing
Till earth and heaven ring
Ring with the harmonies of Liberty;

let our rejoicing rise,
high as the list'ning skies, let it resound loud as the rolling sea
sing a song full of faith that the dark past has tought us,
sing a song full of the hope that the present has brought us;
facing the rising sun of our new day begun,
let us march on till victory is won.

Stony the road we trod,
bitter the chast'ning rod,
felt in the day that hope unborn had died;
yet with a steady beat,
have not our weary feet,
come to the place on witch our fathers sighed?
we have come over a way that with tears has been watered,
we have come, treading our path through the blood of the slaughtered,
out from the gloomy past, till now we stand at last
where the white gleam of our star is cast.

God of our weary years,
God of our silent tears,
thou who has brought us thus far on the way;
thou who has by thy might,
led us into the light,
keep us forever in the path, we pray
lest our feet stray frm the places, our God, where we met thee,
least our hearts, drunk with the wine of the world, we forget thee,
shadowed beneath the hand,
may we forever stand,
tru to our God,
Tru to our native land.

Ms. Camisha and her sister, Ms. LaTanya stood to address the visitors. The sisters excused the children so that everyone could begin the activities for the evening.

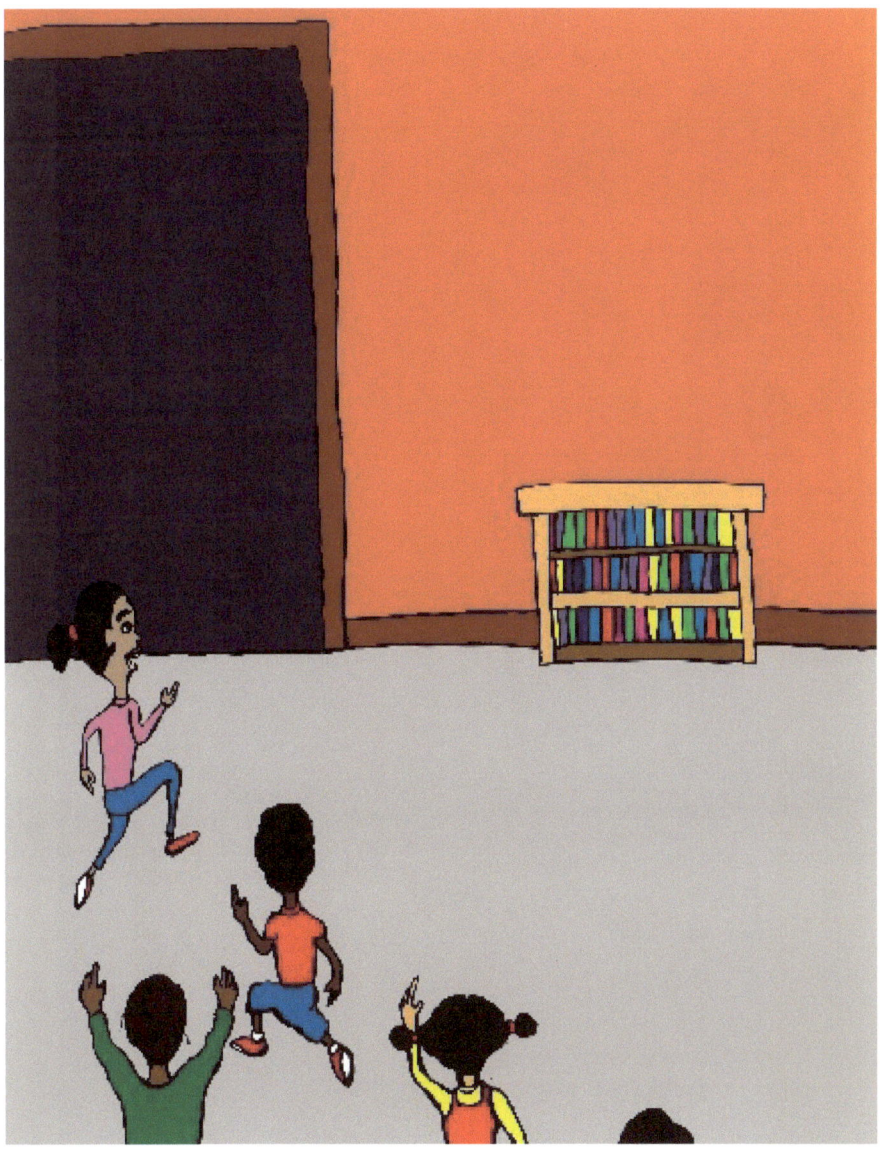

The children joined Sonorra in the kitchen area. Immediately, the children began asking tons of questions. They began grabbing paper, markers, paint, glitter, and other supplies. They were speaking loudly and all at the same time.

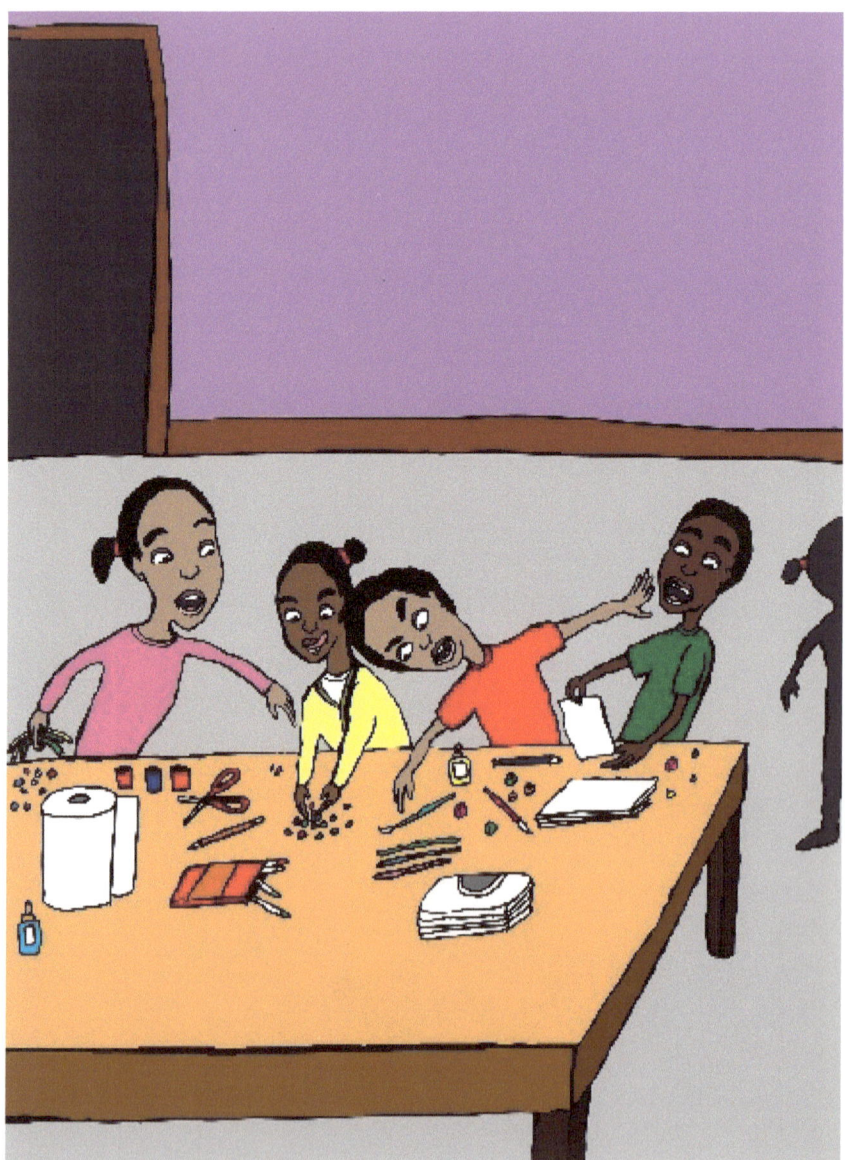

Sonorra shouted, "Habari Gani!"

The children responded, "Ujima".

Sonorra shouted, "Habari Gani!"

The children responded, "Ujima".

Sonorra shouted, "Habari Gani!"

The children responded, "Ujima".

Suddenly the children were silent. They continued to smile. Some looked on with bulging eyes and curiosity. Others looked annoyed. They simply wanted to socialize and indulge in the art supplies.

Sonorra began to speak.

"Now that I have your attention, I want to let you know what we are going to do this evening. We are going to work around Ujima. We will work collectively to create a book."

The children pooh-poohed the idea.

"We can't make no book!" someone shouted.

"But how can we make a book? Mosaiah asked.

Sonorra responded, "I'll type and you talk, and before you know it, we'll have a book, but remember, the discussion has to center around collective works and responsibility. Also, we have to address ways to remain safe at home, at school, and in the community."

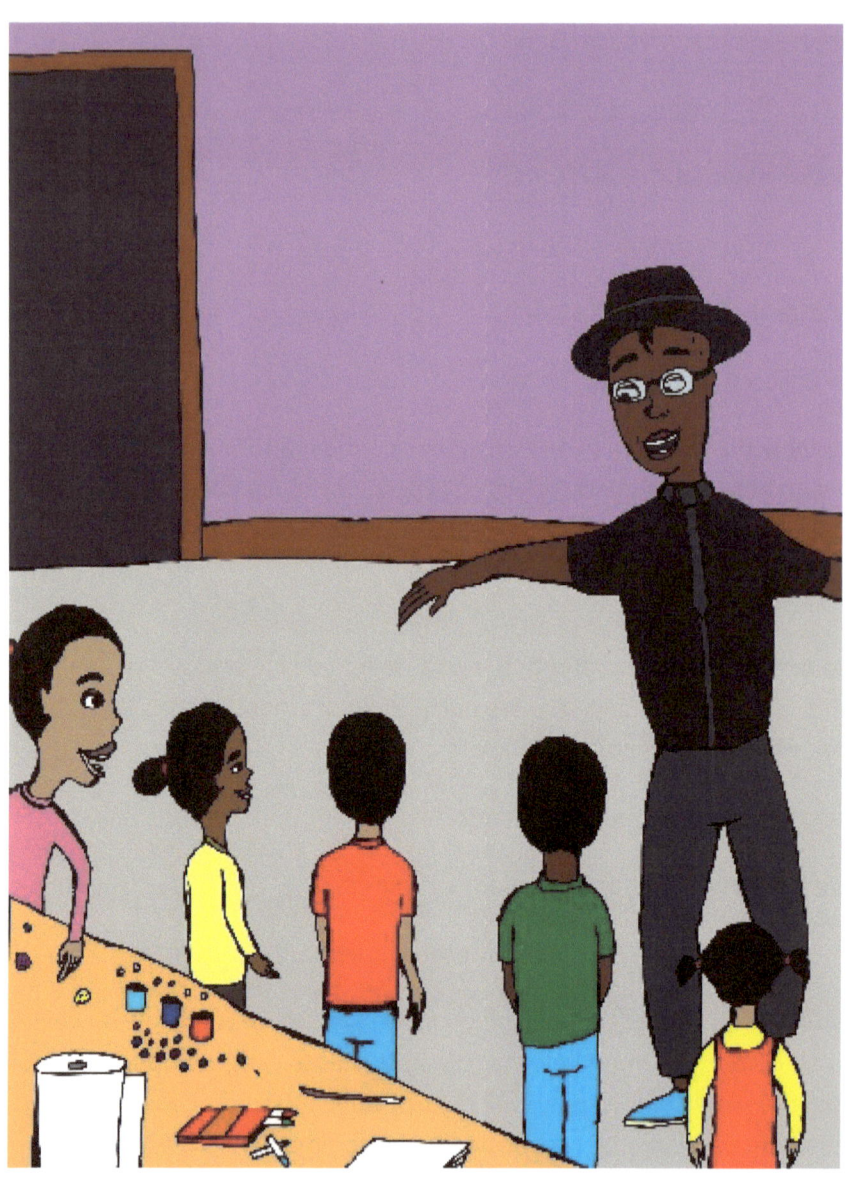

The children looked at one another, then back at Sonorra, and back at one another again.

Mosaiah picked up a piece of paper, folded, and cut it into quarter pieces.

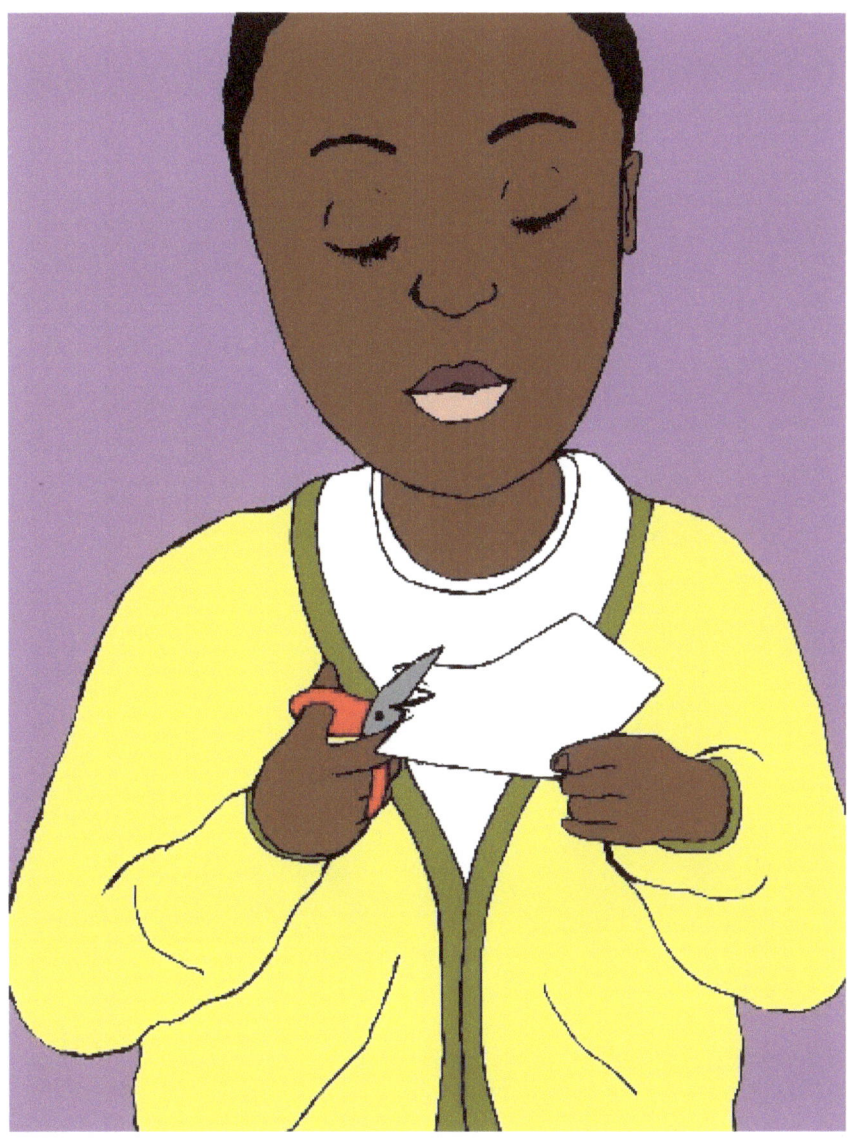

"Here!" Somebody can have my book! Mosaiah shouted.

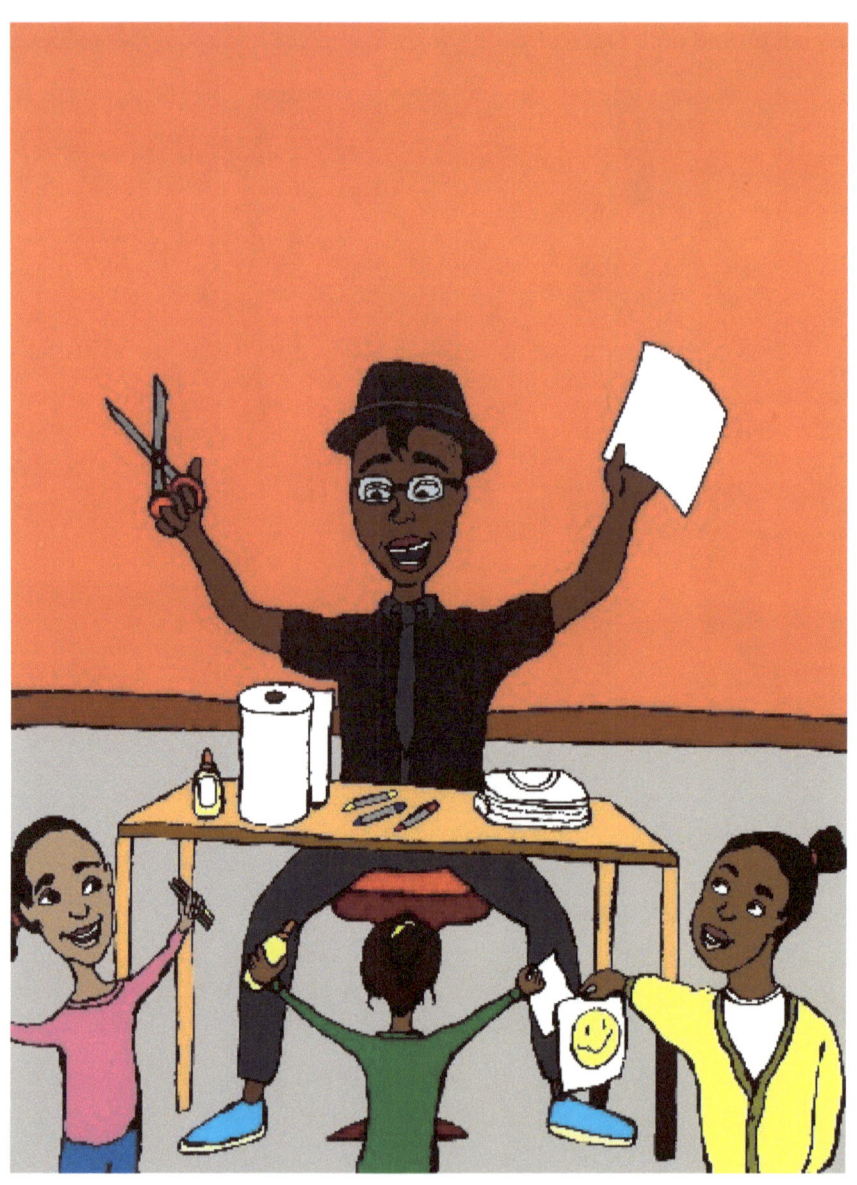

Sonorra responded, "Why thank you Mosaiah." Sonorra looked through
the pages of Mosaiah's book, but there were no words. Sonorra smiled
and said, "That is a beautiful picture book, but we want to include
everyone and add words. Let's begin our book collectively. You hold onto
that book for future use Mosaiah. I'll start us off."

Sonorra began typing and reading aloud. The children began to move closer to see if Sonorra was truly typing. Sonorra said, "Once upon a time there lived a little girl named…."

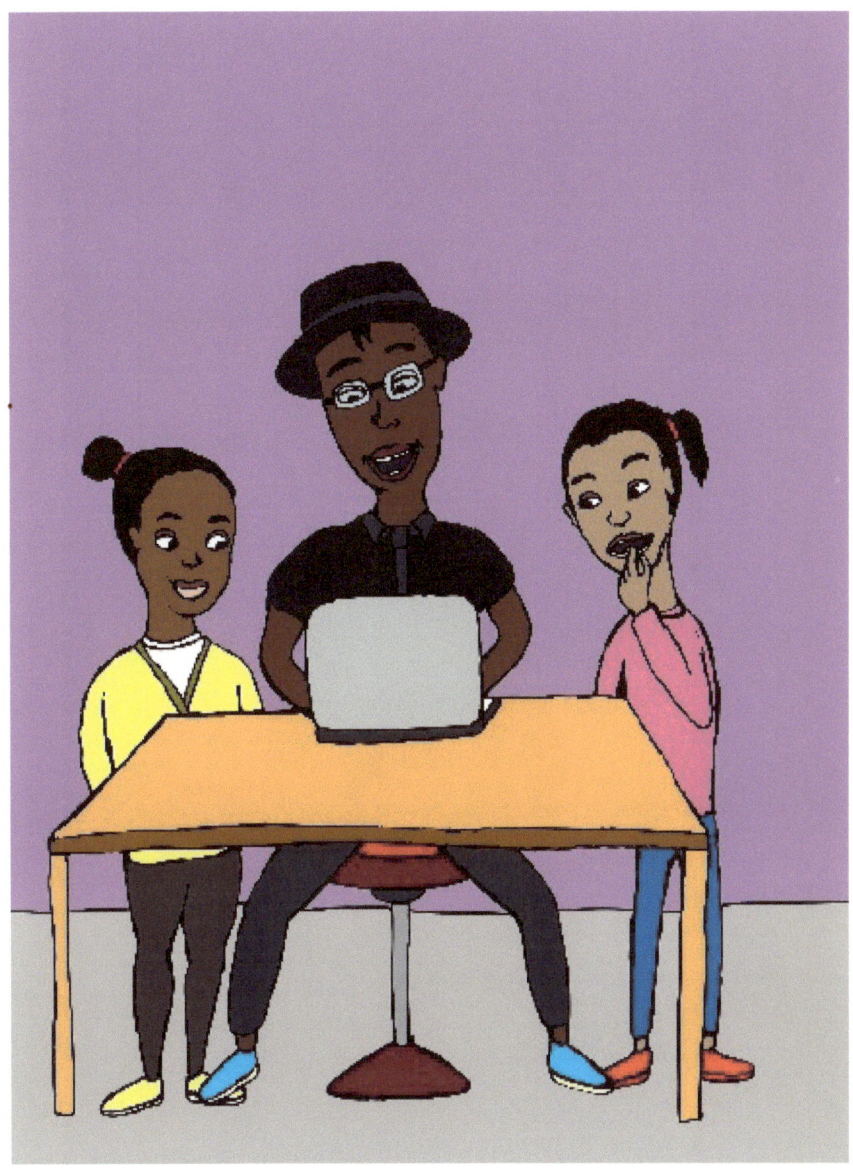

The children slowly began to fill in the blanks. They took turns sharing lines and completing one another's sentences.

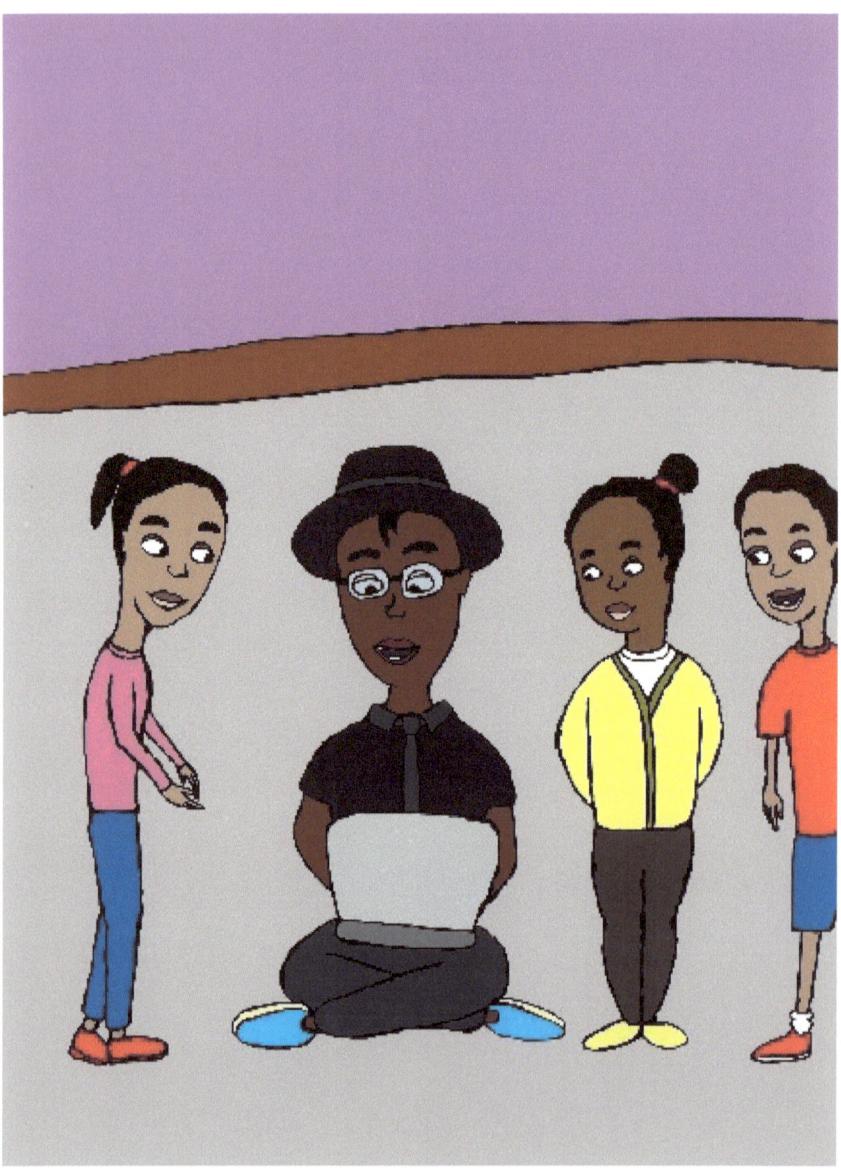

Once upon a time there lived a little girl named Breonna Nared. Breonna had nice friends to play with her. One day, Breonna and her family came to Life Enrichment Bookstore for a Kwanzaa dinner and celebration with the community.

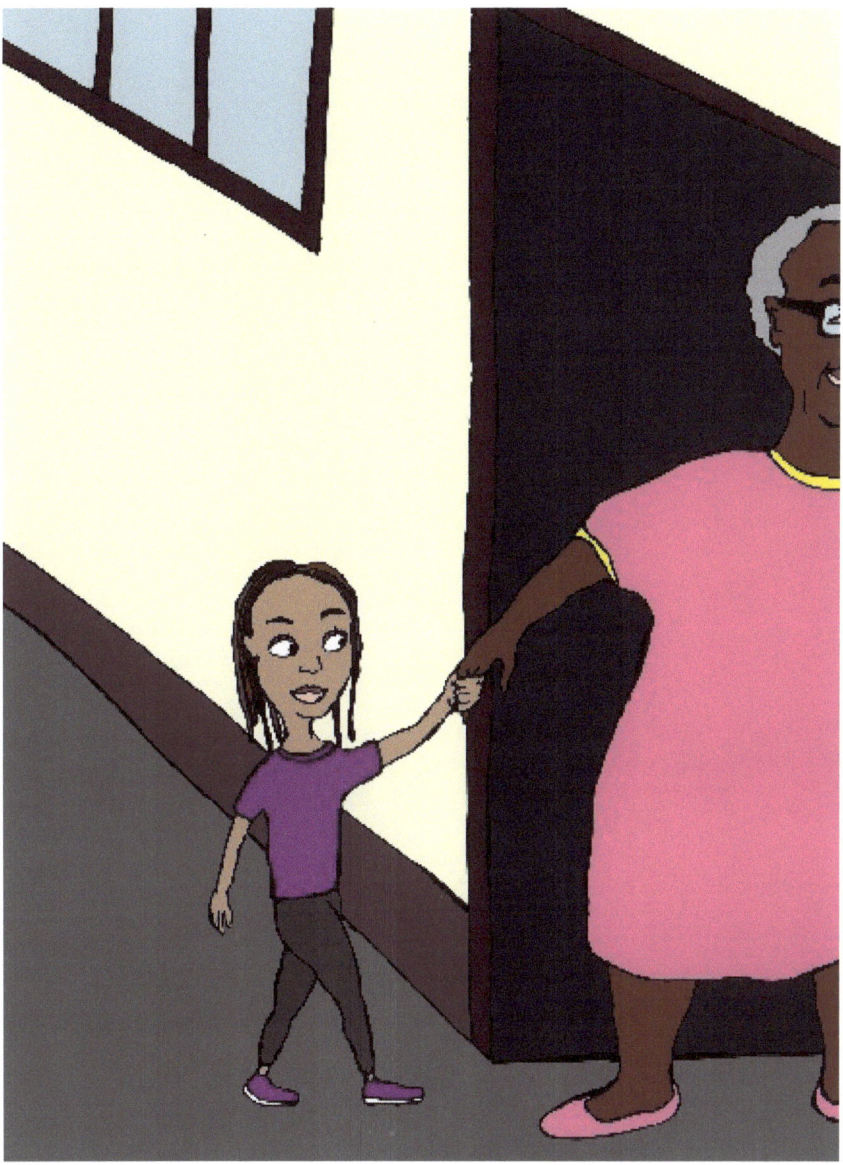

Mosaiah came to life enrichment bookstore with her family as well.

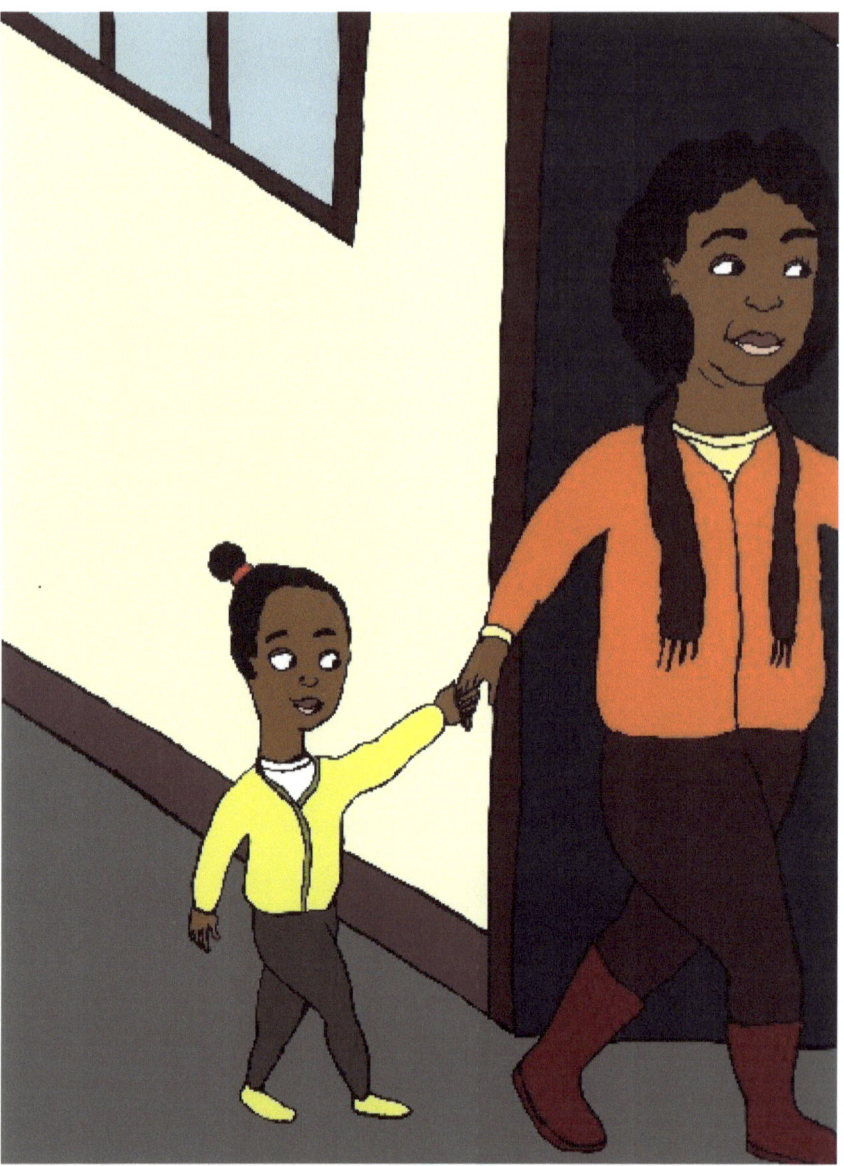

Mosaiah began bullying Breonna. Latricia yelled, Stop that! You're being a bully!" Deshae said please don't bully Breonna. Just have fun.

Mosaiah was not happy that the children scolded her for behaving irresponsibly, so she continued the aggressive behavior. All the children started fighting with Mosaiah, because she kept bullying.

They fought, and they fought, and they fought.

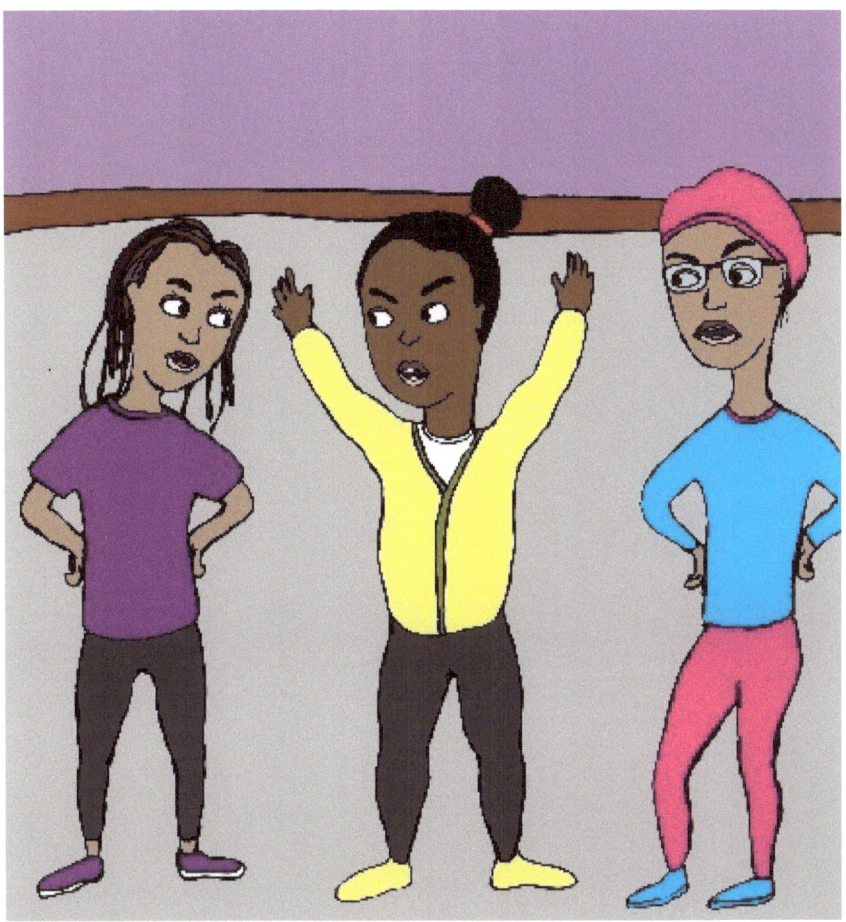

The elders noticed the commotion and looked on with discontent.

Ms Vickie said, "Their problems are our problems, and we need to collectively decide how to stop them from ever fighting again."

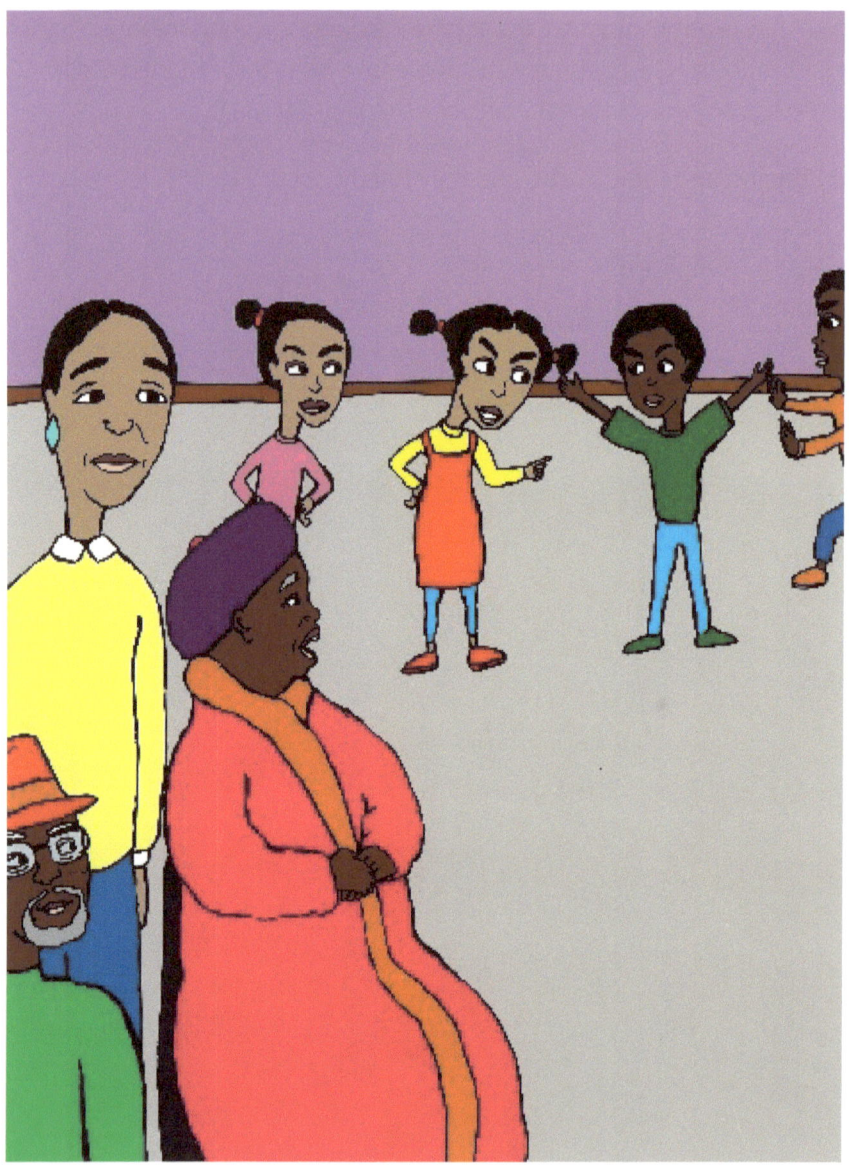

The adults agreed to let the children resolve their problems without adult interference.

The adults gradually departed. Ms. Vickie shut off all the lights and locked the doors. After some time the children realized it was dark and all the adults had gone home. The children were stuck. They could not leave, and they were very tired from fighting. They had no choice. They slept over at the Life Enrichment Bookstore.

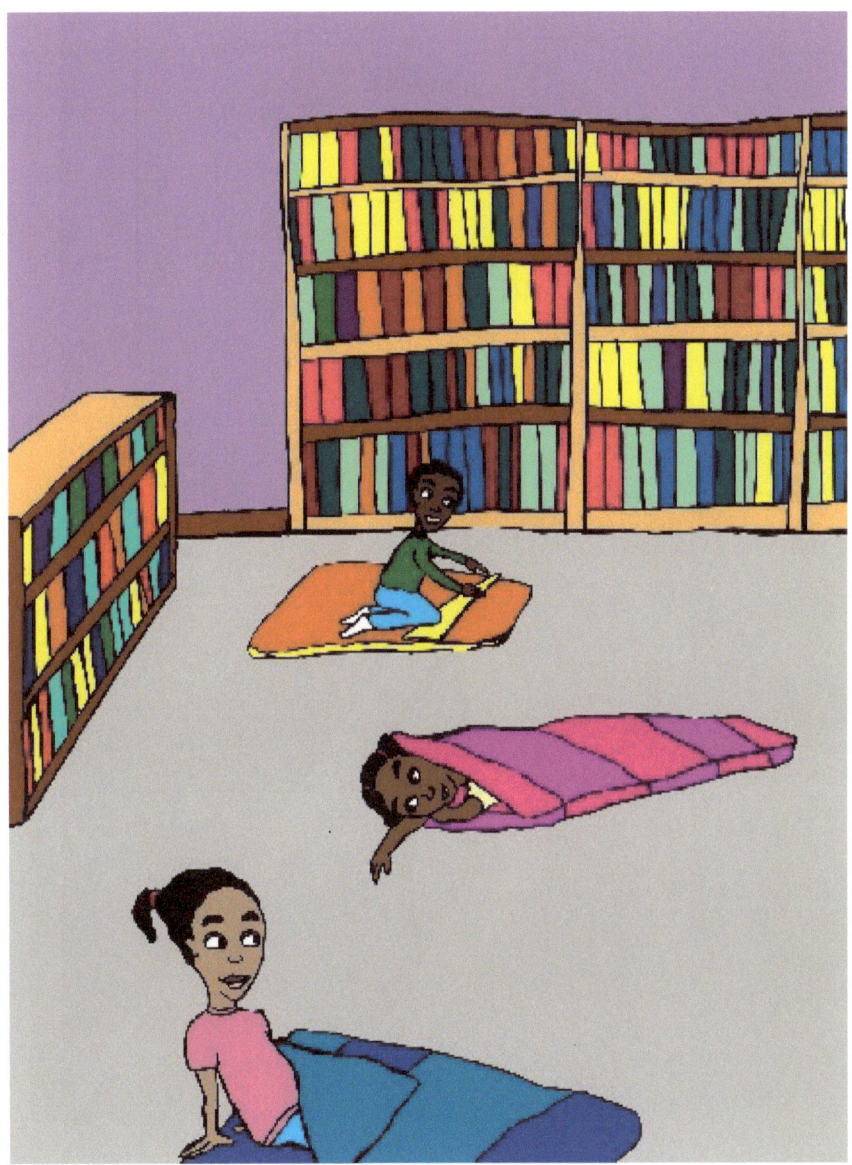

The children were not aware that Sonorra had agreed to stay with the children over night. Sonorra woke up early the next morning to unlock the bookstore. Sonorra went outside, stretched, and took in some fresh air.

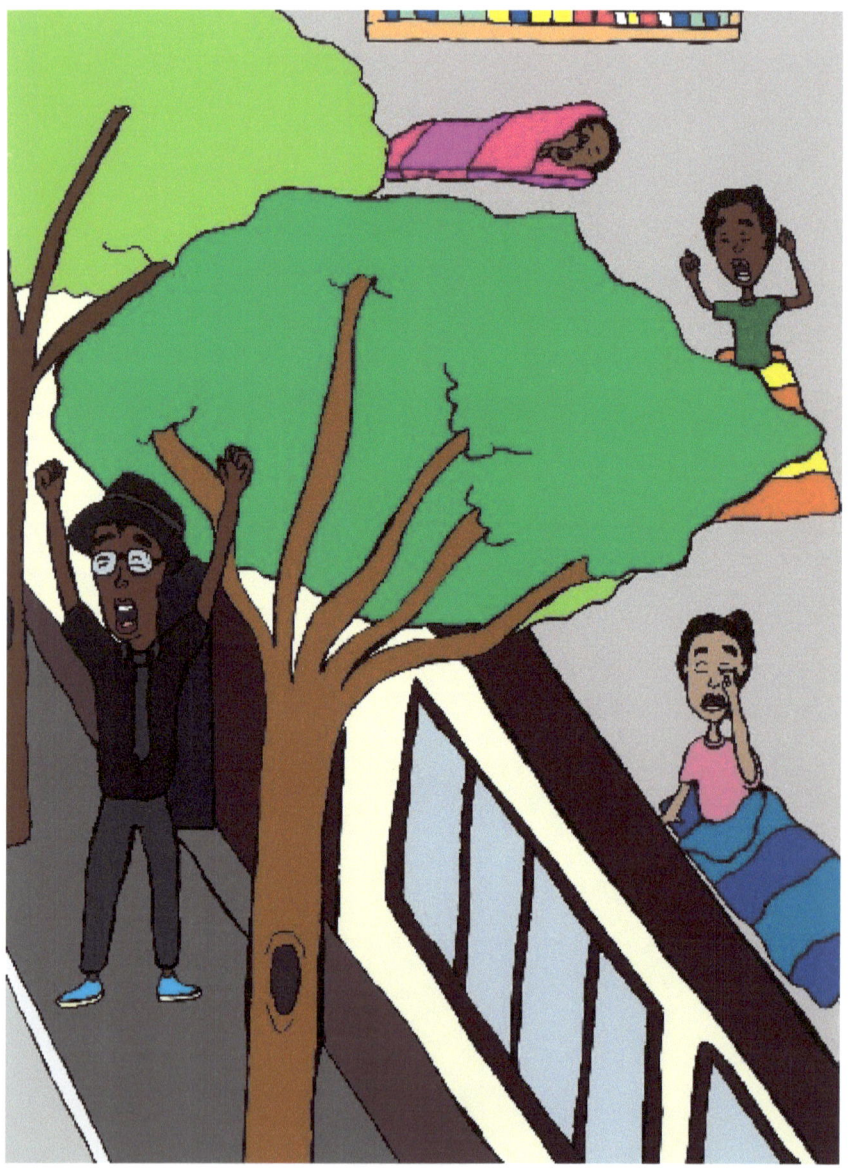

Sonorra reentered the bookstore and made loud noises as to awaken the children.

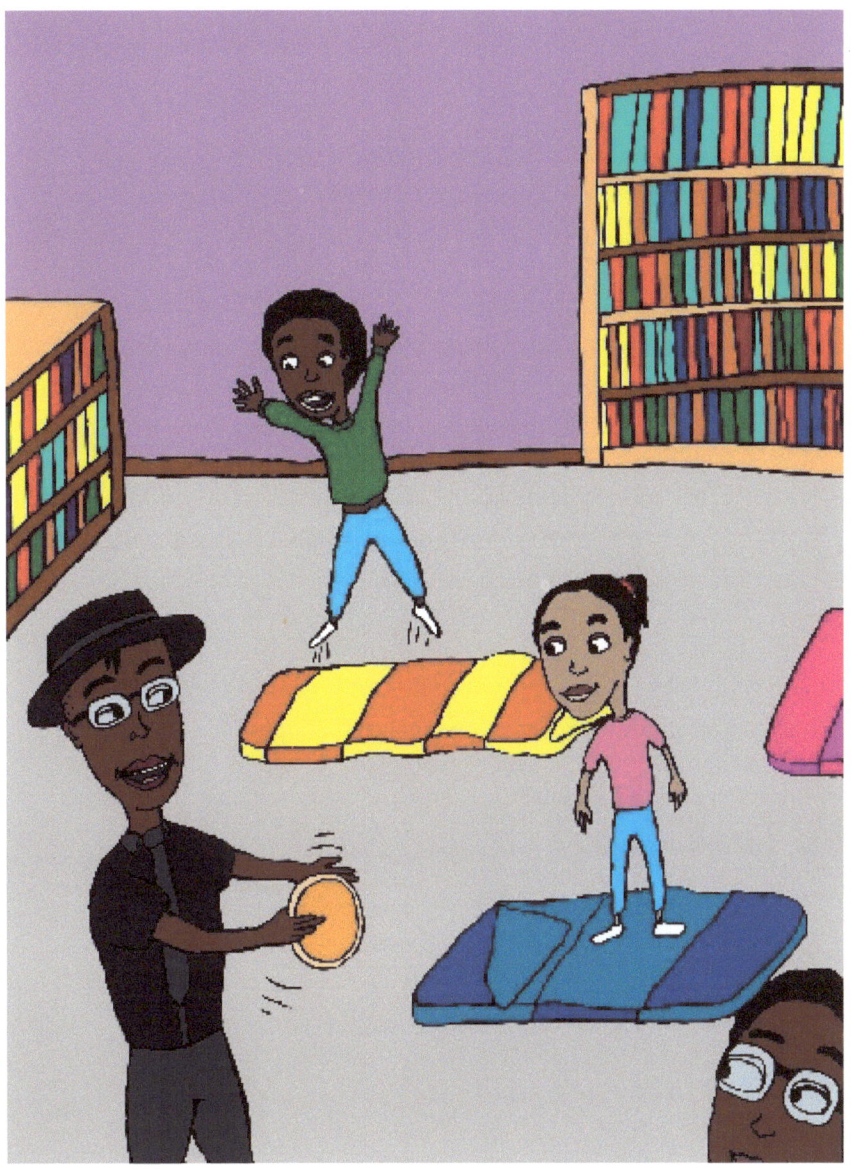

The children were very excited to see an adult. They told Sonorra all about their fighting.

Sonorra knew about the fighting. She watched and listened the entire time from another space in the building. As a matter of fact, Sonorra had not slept at all. She watched over each child all through the night to ensure their safety. She also pondered her approach to dealing with the fighting.

Sonorra smiled and said, "In the spirit of Ujima and the 7 Kwanzaa principles, we need to talk about how to handle something like this in the future."

Naylani began sharing. "My grandma is always like, talking it out makes it better, because it's not violent. If somebody doesn't like what you say, you just walk away. This girl said if you don't give me a cookie I'm not going to be your friend. I didn't like what she said, so I walked away."

Fanikia said, "My mom's been talking about emotional abuse for years and also I've learned it because I've been through that; when you have emotions and you feel like you're being abused or somebody is being mean."

Mosaiah said, "That makes me sad to hear that story." Naylani said, "That's messed up that somebody has to go through that."

Breonna said, "Have fun don't be mean and stop bullying. Have fun!"

The children all agreed that Breonna was right. They all became friends and agreed never to hurt one another or anyone else again.

They all shouted, "UJIMA!" and gathered for one big hug.

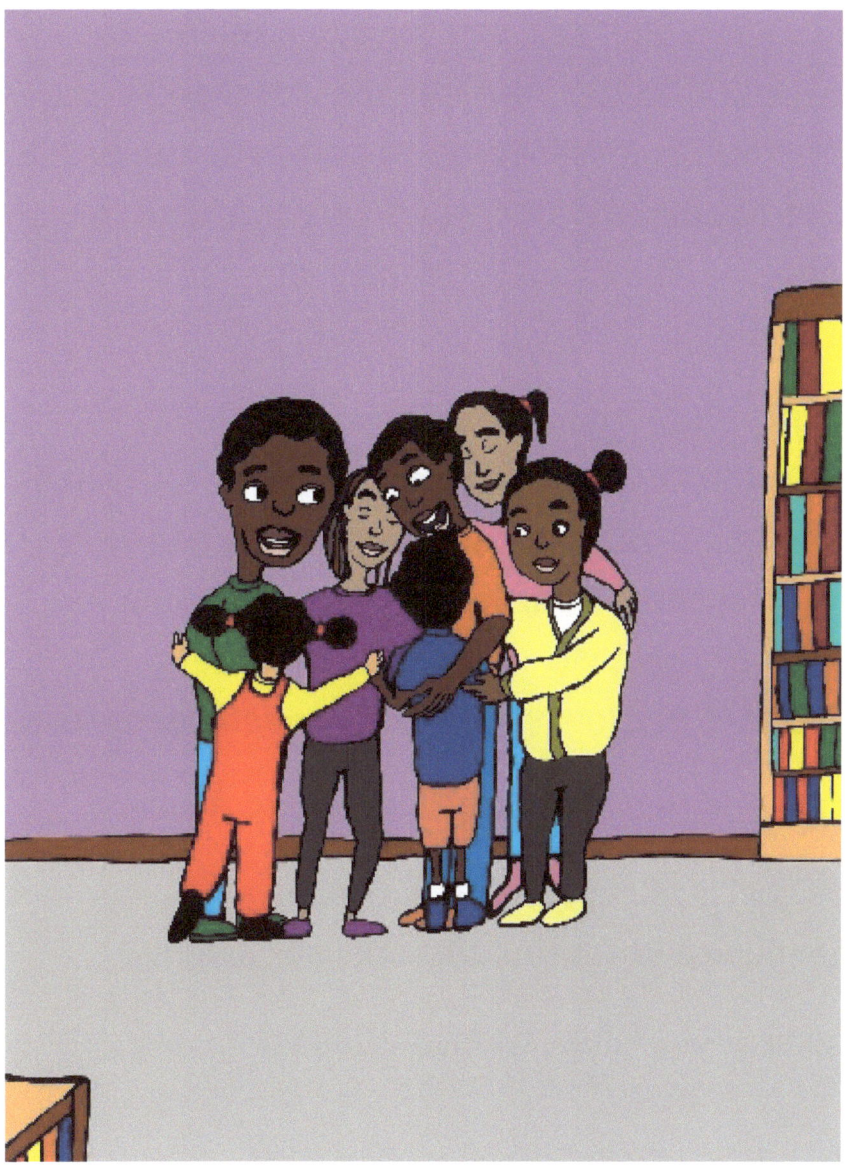

Parents/Facilitators: Please put down the book for a discussion. Once everyone has a clear understanding of the identified topic, pick-up the book and discuss Kwanzaa; family, public, and community violence; and ways to remain safe. Ensure you address levels of individual and collective responsibilities. You may also utilize this space to address family traditions and ways to honor your ancestors in keeping with the Kwanzaa traditions.

It is important to include all members in the discussion. Ensure all members are heard. One person or all parties may write. If only one person writes, ensure all parties share their information out loud. Creativity is important, but not as important as a loving, respectful, open discussion.

There are no bad questions or wrong answers.

The goal is to generate open, honest communication without shaming or judgment.

Highlight your discussion or adjust the story on the lines provided.

ABOUT THE AUTHOR

Sonorra is a blogger and social activist. She is the founder of Shades N Love and Co-owner of Shades N Love Incorporated LLC. She provides life skills coaching, education, and consultation, as well as presents at conferences and public speaking engagements.

Sonorra retired from the U.S. Army after serving in Operations Desert Storm/Shield, Joint Endeavor, and Iraqi/Enduring Freedom. She graduated from Chapman
University, with a Masters degree in Psychology, with an emphasis in Marriage and Family Therapy.

Sonorra has provided residential mental health services, juvenile delinquency, chemical dependency, eating disorders, and religious abuse. She has advocated for the safety of children and women who endured domestic abuse, sexual assault, and/or child abuse, as well as for service members who suffer from PTSD.

Sonorra is the author of a series of children's book that contains characters with "ethnic" names, and shades of color designed primarily for the LGBTQ community.

"Empowering others and increasing unity through open, honest communication regarding civil rights issues of every variation is paramount."

Look for other great books written by Sonorra McMath, available at Life Enrichment Bookstore and Createspace.com.

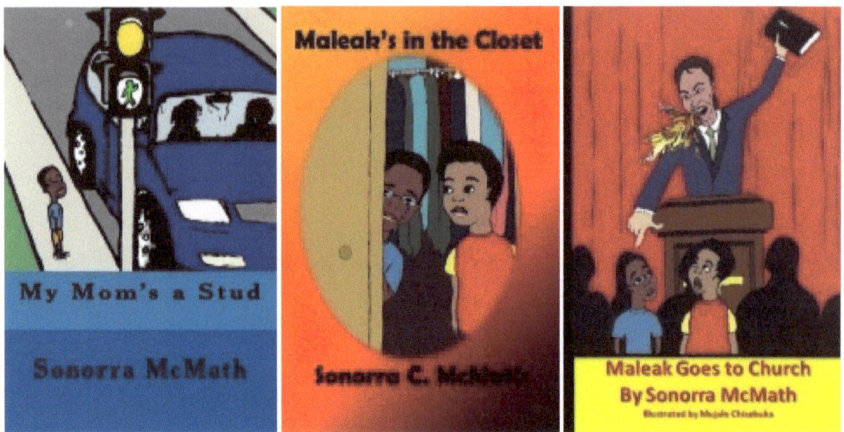

Contact Sonorra directly at Sonorra@comcast.net. Forward your completed workbook section to the author to have it incorporated into the story. We will edit and reprint your version of the story and make it available for purchase. All submitted materials become the sole property of the company.